PASTICHE was originally presented at the University of Georgia's Laboratory Theatre under the supervision of Dr. Leighton M. Ballew. The stage manager was Jim Hampton and the dresser Elaine Glascoe. The play was directed by David Shelton, with the following cast:

MEDFORD .... *Ted Harris*

LADY ALEXANDRA .... *Judy McKinnon*

SIR PETER .... *Gilbert Lee*

VIOLA .... *Susu Williams*

PASTICHE was previously published, in a reading version, by the DeKalb Literary Arts Journal, Volume III, Number 1, in 1968.

CW00517003

3

CHARACTERS

Sir Peter Tanford, aged about 50

Lady Alexandra Tanford, 45

Viola Vionysse, 22

Medford, 25

SETTING

Sir Peter's elegant town house in London

Note: Some of the costume changes are deliberately written to be fast. Part of the fun is that MEDFORD's changes into, out of, and back into the policeman are rushed and frantic.

Pastiche

(A small, elegant sitting-room, late at night. At rise,
MEDFORD, *a harrassed young man in ill-fitting
butler's togs, is rather frantically laying a small
table, center, for two. He arranges a cold supper,
sets a vase of flowers, and places a bottle of
champagne in a vast silver ice-bucket in the
center of the table. He is then, with the help of
a large etiquette book, trying to get the silverware
correct, when* LADY ALEXANDRA, *a beautiful
woman of about forty-five, wearing a superb
evening gown, comes into the room.)*

ALEX. Oh 'Evening, Medford.

MEDFORD. *(Dropping something.)* Good evening,
m'lady.

ALEX. Is Timothy still ill?

MEDFORD. Yes, m'lady. Sir Peter asked me to lay
supper and wait up for him. Do you know where these
go, m'lady? *(Holding silverware.)*

ALEX. Yes, on the right.

MEDFORD. Thank you.

ALEX. I'm so glad I came back. I knew he'd remember.

MEDFORD. *(Puzzled.)* Excuse me?

ALEX. It's such a lovely night. Don't you think so?

MEDFORD. If you say so, m'lady.

ALEX. I was at Moira Temple's come as you were
party, being bored to death by Rodney Howard, who
insisted on telling me about his mother's goiter till
I wished she'd choke on it, and when he'd finished

5

that, along with far too many drinks, he started telling
me all about his noisy Italian sports car, and quite
suddenly I thought of the little, old car Noddy had
when we were married. Then, of course, I remembered.

MEDFORD. (*Completely lost.*) Of course, m'lady.

ALEX. I suppose I've ruined everything by coming
home too soon. What time is it?

MEDFORD. Eleven-thirty, m'lady.

ALEX. Well, if I'd been any later it wouldn't have
been our anniversary. But that doesn't matter, does it?

MEDFORD. The least of our problems, m'lady.

ALEX. What?

MEDFORD. (*Quickly.*) Congratulations, m'lady.

ALEX. Why thank you, Medford. Twenty-five years.
I've been in love for a quarter of a century. And do
you know, in all that time, Noddy's never said, in so
many words, I love you. I sometime's wonder. (*Pause.*)

MEDFORD. I think . . . that . . . perhaps . . .

ALEX. (*Continuing.*) I thought Noddy might turn up
with some predatory little chorus girl. Silly really.
We've remained quite stubbornly faithful. After all,
Noddy's not the type to run around with chorus girls.

MEDFORD. No, m'lady.

ALEX. Is he expecting me to be here, or to come in
later?

MEDFORD. I don't think, m'lady, that he's expecting
you at all.

ALEX. What?

MEDFORD. Someone else.

ALEX. But there's no one else who'd want to cele-
brate my anniversary with me.

MEDFORD. I mean . . . that is, Sir Peter is enter-
taining someone else. If you see what I mean.

ALEX. Thank you, yes. It was brutally succinct.

MEDFORD. I can easily get you a little cold supper, m'lady.

ALEX. (*Ice.*) With whom is Peter dining tonight?

MEDFORD. (*A suggestion.*) Lord Durham?

ALEX. Try not to be offensive, Medford.

MEDFORD. Yes, m'lady. Perhaps Sir Peter's mother?

ALEX. They haven't spoken since he married above himself, twenty-five years ago. I would like a resumé of the entire squalid situation.

MEDFORD. May I speak openly, m'lady?

ALEX. Openly, but not freely.

MEDFORD. Well, you see, you've been going to all these parties and . . .

ALEX. I'm extremely well-informed about what I've been doing. The subject is my apparently errant, aging husband.

MEDFORD. He's been seeing a chorus girl. (*Slight pause.*)

ALEX. You're the only person I ever told of my worries about Noddy. And no sooner have I spoken, than it's true. Twenty-five years. It's rather sad.

MEDFORD. She's very petty.

ALEX. Spare me the seamier sides of the story.

MEDFORD. Yes, m'lady.

ALEX. Just how long has . . .

MEDFORD. Three weeks.

ALEX. Three.

MEDFORD. Only one or two meetings, I think.

ALEX. Just how far has . . .

MEDFORD. Far, m'lady?

ALEX. If you force me to be explicit, Medford, I shall discharge you on the spot.

MEDFORD. Well, to be blunt . .

ALEX. Don't be.

MEDFORD. So far . . . nothing untoward has happened.

ALEX. You mean it's not too late?

MEDFORD. Well, the situation is repairable. But things are . . .

ALEX. Deteriorating?

MEDFORD. That depends on one's point of view, m'lady.

ALEX. How far have things progressed?

MEDFORD. (*Indicating table.*) To supper, and they're going to be here any minute.

ALEX. What are they having? (*Picks up champagne.*) Oh, dear. Of all the cruel, thoughtless things to do.

MEDFORD. M'lady?

ALEX. This is the last bottle of a case I was given when Peter and I were married. Change it.

MEDFORD. For anything in particular?

ALEX. How about Dry Sac.

MEDFORD. Yes, m'lady.

ALEX. What's her name?

MEDFORD. Viola Vionysse.

ALEX. Really.

MEDFORD. No, really it's Avis Phelps.

ALEX. How appropriate. What on earth are we going to do?

MEDFORD. Hire a private detective, m'lady.

ALEX. Private detectives produce public information.

MEDFORD. You could just throw her out.

ALEX. Noddy's misplaced sense of chivalry would defeat us there.

MEDFORD. Disguise yourself as a Salvation Army Officer, and surprise them.

ALEX. Is there nothing to do that won't reduce the whole situation to a farce?

MEDFORD. Nothing, m'lady.

ALEX. Oh, dear. We shall just have to fight foolishness with foolishness.

MEDFORD. You'd better hurry, m'lady. You don't want to be trapped and have to hide under the table.

ALEX. That kind of foolishness is completely out of the question. Now this must be a joint endeavor.

MEDFORD. I have my loyalty to Sir Peter to think of, m'lady. He promoted me from boot-boy. And, after all ethically . . .

ALEX. This is no time for ethics. Now change the wine, while I think. We mustn't let them be alone together. How do we do it?

MEDFORD. Disguises.

ALEX. Oh, very well. Now hurry.

MEDFORD. (*Taking bottle and going to door.*) There's some costumes in the attic. Here they are!

ALEX. What?

MEDFORD. Them.

ALEX. Where?

MEDFORD. Here!

ALEX. Help!

MEDFORD. Hide!

ALEX. Where?

MEDFORD. Under the table. (*Pause.*)

ALEX. Don't be ridiculous, Medford.

MEDFORD. Lady Alexandra, please.

ALEX. (*Bitterly.*) I wish I were drunk.

MEDFORD. Later, m'lady.

ALEX. (*Getting under table.*) What do I do under here?

MEDFORD. Recite Swinbourne, m'lady. (*He starts to the door, remembers something, grabs the wine, and hands it to* LADY ALEXANDRA. *He has just straightened up when the door opens.* SIR PETER, *a handsome man of about fifty, and* VIOLA VIONYSSE, *a pretty chorus girl, enter.)*

PETER. 'Evening, Medford.

MEDFORD. Good evening, Sir Peter.

PETER. All set?

MEDFORD. Yes sir.

PETER. Fine, that'll be all thank you, Medford.

MEDFORD. Do you find it too hot in here, Sir Peter?

PETER. No, it feels pleasant.

MEDFORD. Too cold, perhaps?

PETER. No, why?

MEDFORD. I just thought you might be more comfortable in the dining room.

PETER. The dining room's so large.

MEDFORD. Exactly. None of this . . . oppressive intimacy.

PETER. I think we have everything we need, thank you Medford.

MEDFORD. (*As he leaves.*) The drawing room?

PETER. That's all, Medford! (MEDFORD *exits.*) Well . . .

VIOLA. Yes?

PETER. Nothing. (*Pause.*)

VIOLA. Nice house.

PETER. Thank you.

VIOLA. My friend Rose said she knew you was quality, 'cause of the address. You can always tell.

MEDFORD. (*Sticking his head in.*) How about the kitchen? Very cosy. (*Exits.*)

PETER. NO! (*To* VIOLA.) The butler's ill. We've had to promote Medford suddenly. He's training.

VIOLA. I could tell he was common, right away.

PETER. Shall we eat?

VIOLA. I'm famished.

PETER. Vichyssoise?

VIOLA. I beg your pardon?

PETER. Soup?

VIOLA. Don't mind if I do.

PETER. There you are.

VIOLA. This is ever so nice.

PETER. Delicious isn't it.

VIOLA. I mean being here.

PETER. Yes. Well, I am often.

VIOLA. I suppose so.

PETER. Of course, I live here.

VIOLA. I meant, the two of us. Me and a knight.

PETER. What?

VIOLA. Me and a knight. With a K.

PETER. Oh, you mean me and me. You and I.

VIOLA. Yes.

PETER. What about it?

VIOLA. It's ever so nice.

PETER. What?

VIOLA. Being here. (*Pause.*) Have you got a castle?

PETER. No, 'fraid not.

VIOLA. Do you mind.

PETER. Not much. They're awfully hard to keep clean.

VIOLA. I think I'm disappointed.

PETER. About not having a castle?

VIOLA. Yes, do you know what I mean?

PETER. Yes, I do. I must confess . . . I'm a little disappointed myself.

VIOLA. But you said you didn't mind because they're hard to keep clean.

PETER. No, I mean I think I'm disappointed you didn't wear the dress you wear in the show.

VIOLA. Which one?

PETER. The white one.

VIOLA. It'd look silly in the street.

PETER. It's beautiful on stage.

VIOLA. It doesn't really fit. My friend Rose says it's an old-fashioned show what with castles and princesses and everyone waltzing all over the place. 'Course it is corny, but I've got to eat, and I suppose somebody likes it.

PETER. Yes. I do. (*Pause.*)

VIOLA. You're not your usual self, tonight.

PETER. I'm in an unusual situation.

VIOLA. I remember the first time we met, in that teashop, and you said that in the play I was like a dream you'd had for years. That was ever such a lovely thing to say.

PETER. It was true.

VIOLA. And here we are. In love. I've dreamed of something like this too. Rose says dreaming helps to pass the night.

PETER. I'm much older than you.

VIOLA. That's all right. You know how I think of you?

PETER. How?

VIOLA. *Trés distinque.* That's French.

PETER. Yes. I know. Excuse me.

VIOLA. I beg your pardon?

PETER. I just kicked you.

VIOLA. No, you didn't.

PETER. Well, I certainly kicked something.

VIOLA. Probably the table leg.

PETER. The table has a very soft leg then. (*He starts under table.*)

VIOLA. (*Stopping him.*) Sir Peter?

PETER. Yes?

VIOLA. Why did you ask me here tonight?

PETER. For supper.

VIOLA. Why not your wife?

PETER. She's away for the weekend.

VIOLA. I don't suppose you see much of each other. Do you have separate bedrooms?

PETER. Why?

VIOLA. Just wondered. I mean if you've been married for years and years and all. I mean, I thought you might.

PETER. Have you had enough soup?

VIOLA. Yes, thanks ever so.

PETER. There's no wine.

VIOLA. Do you remember our first supper?

PETER. Yes, that unsavory, subterranean coffee-shop.

VIOLA. Where they had that marvellous two-fingered guitar player.

PETER. And that oily waitress with the slave bangle in her ear. I wonder if it hurts.

VIOLA. What?

PETER. Having your ears pierced. Are yours?

VIOLA. (*Taking off an earring.*) No, these just clip on. See. (*She drops it.*)

PETER. I'll get it. (*Gets on hands and knees.*)

VIOLA. Got it?

PETER. Not yet.

VIOLA. Maybe it's over this side. (*Gets on hands and knees.*) I don't see it.

PETER. Perhaps it went under the table. (*Starts to lift tablecloth.*)

VIOLA. No, I saw it bounce away.

PETER. This is ridiculous. (*They are both kneeling back to back several feet apart.*)

VIOLA. It's very small.

PETER. It can't have gone far.

VIOLA. It's not very valuable.

PETER. Here it is. (*He holds it out to her, backwards, because in the process of getting up he is dusting the knees of his trousers.*)

VIOLA. Oh, good. It was a present from Rose. (*She

turns on her knees to get it, reaches out for it, nearly overbalances, turns back to grab the table or her chair. In the moment that they are poised back to back, with arms outstretched, LADY ALEXANDRA *takes the earring from* PETER *and puts one of her own in* VIOLA's *hand. They stand up and turn in. Both momentarily register the fact that they could not have reached each other.*) Thank you.

PETER. You know I planned a lovely, romantic supper, and it's just not working.

VIOLA. I'm enjoying it. Really I am. Rose says never judge a dinner till you've had dessert.

PETER. I wish we'd gone somewhere else.

VIOLA. This is a lovely room.

PETER. I know, but the knowledge that it used to be the nursery reduces its amorous atmosphere immensely.

VIOLA. Your nursery?

PETER. No, my children's. I should have met you twenty years ago.

VIOLA. I was only two years old.

PETER. Then I should never have met you at all. I should never have seen that absurd show or heard you sing that insipid song.

VIOLA. Which song?

PETER. You know, the one on the balcony. When the prince sings. (*Sings. They assume elaborately artificial poses in front of the table.* PETER *is on one knee. They sing in the manner of an old operetta.*)

Time and place,
Can not erase,
My memory of you.
Though far away,
This fading day,
To me will still be new.

(*Artificially.*) My beloved, I must leave tonight. I must leave you forever.

VIOLA. When you're in love, forever is only a moment, and a moment is forever. And though you go a thousand miles away, I'll come to you. (VIOLA *joins in.*)

I'll come to you
And in your dreams
Although it seems
As if we're far apart
I'll come to you
And in your dreams
I'll give to you
   My heart.

(*During the song the table moves backwards to the door.* LADY ALEXANDRA *stands and exits with the champagne.* MEDFORD *enters with new bottle and pushes the table back to its original position. They end the song.*)

MEDFORD. Your wine, sir.

PETER. Oh . . . er . . . thank you, Medford.

MEDFORD. Anything the matter, Sir Peter?

PETER. No. I was going to leave forever, and Miss Vionysse was planning to come to me.

MEDFORD. Very amusing, sir.

PETER. It's not like that at all, dammit.

MEDFORD. Would you like me to serve, Sir Peter?

PETER. No, I'll serve.

MEDPORD. Would you like me to uncork the wine, Sir Peter?

PETER. No, I'll uncork it.

MEDFORD. Would you like anything else, Sir Peter?

PETER. Yes, I'd like you to help me up.

MEDFORD. Oops! There we are. We've got to watch that lumbago, haven't we.

PETER. One of us will be enough, thank you.

MEDFORD. Yes, Sir Peter. (*He remains, watching.*)

PETER. Shall we sit at the table?

VIOLA. Oh, very well.

PETER. Champagne?

VIOLA. Well, I won't say no.

PETER. What?

MEDFORD. She means yes.

PETER. You can go, Medford.

MEDFORD. Thank you, sir. (*Exits.*)

VIOLA. Well, here we are alone at last. This is ever so cosy. I feel quite at home.

PETER. Really?

VIOLA. You know what I mean?

PETER. At ease?

VIOLA. Yes. You know how to put things, don't you? Rose says look for a man who knows how to put things and you'll find a man who says what he means.

PETER. Very pithy.

VIOLA. Yes, well, she is.

PETER. Who?

VIOLA. Rose.

PETER. What?

VIOLA. Pithy.

PETER. I think I'm beginning to hate your friend Rose.

VIOLA. You shouldn't do that. I mean she fixed things up for us didn't she?

PETER. Did she?

VIOLA. Yes, she certainly did. I was awfully worried about coming here tonight. What with you a married man and me a single girl. Rose said do you like him and I said yes.

PETER. Thank you.

VIOLA. Of course we're being healthy about this.

PETER. Healthy?

VIOLA. Talking. Getting it all straightened out beforehand. There's nothing like communication between two lonely people. My friend Rose says Sex isn't everything.

PETER. Very romantic.

VIOLA. Yes, isn't it. She'd love this.

PETER. What?

VIOLA. The two of us alone together. She'd just love to be here.

PETER. She very nearly is.

VIOLA. I've got an idea. Let's turn out the lights.

PETER. Whatever for?

VIOLA. Romantic atmosphere. (*She gets up and switches off the overhead lighting.*) Light the candles. It'll be lovely. (*The room dark except for a dim pool of light around the table.*) There, isn't that nice?

PETER. Very seductive. I can't see my food.

VIOLA. Why don't you take your tie off.

PETER. No, I think I'll leave it on.

VIOLA. You'll feel more relaxed with it off. (*She is trying to take* PETER's *tie off and he is resisting.*)

PETER. Really, I'd much rather leave it . . .

VIOLA. Come on, don't be bashful . . .

PETER. We haven't finished supper yet.

VIOLA. You're just too formal. Nearly got it. (*They are struggling when* MEDFORD, *disguised as a policeman, enters.*)

MEDFORD. (*Shining a flashlight on them.*) All right! All right! What's going on here? On your feet.

VIOLA. Mind your bloomin' business.

MEDFORD. This is my business, young lady. Where's the light switch?

PETER. On the wall. (MEDFORD *switches lights on.*)

MEDFORD. Oh, it's you, Sir Peter. Dreadfully sorry,

sir. Didn't know it was you. I was merely doing my duty. Preserving the peace and . . . (*Trails off.*)

PETER. (*Ice.*) Yes.

MEDFORD. Oh, I didn't know that you and Lady . . . (*Trails off.*)

PETER. This is Avis . . .

VIOLA. Viola.

PETER. Viola Phelps.

VIOLA. Vionysse.

PETER. Viola Vionysse. My aunt.

VIOLA. Niece.

PETER. Niece.

MEDFORD. How do you do, miss?

VIOLA. Very nicely, thank you.

PETER. Medford!

MEDFORD. Sir?

PETER. You're not . . .

MEDFORD. What?

PETER. This is the most horrible evening of my life.

VIOLA. Well, it's not over yet.

MEDFORD. It certainly isn't.

PETER. Can I help you . . . constable?

MEDFORD. Heavens, no, sir. It's our job to help you. The British policeman is ready to help the British citizen when the need . . .

PETER. Just don't be officious, officer.

MEDFORD. Well, you see what happened, sir, was this. Couple of days ago that young butler of yours, what's his name?

PETER. Medford.

MEDFORD. Yes, that's it, Medford. Very likely lad. I recommend him. He'll go a long way.

PETER. Yes, and he'd better start now.

MEDFORD. Well, he said to me that you and Mrs., that is Lady Alexandra, were going to be out of town

for the weekend. So on my rounds tonight I checked
your front door, which was unlocked, peeped inside,
heard noises, decided to investigate, and found . . .

PETER. That I'd changed my plans.

MEDFORD. Yes, indeed, sir.

PETER. This may warn you, constable, not to listen
to servant's gossip. They're very unreliable. In fact,
they're often fired.

MEDFORD. I'll bear that in mind, sir.

PETER. Do.

VIOLA. And don't bother a gentleman like Sir Peter
again. He's a knight, you know.

MEDFORD. Yes, miss. And you . . .

VIOLA. I'm his aunt.

PETER. Niece.

VIOLA. Niece.

MEDFORD. Well, as long as nothing untoward is hap-
pening, Sir Peter, I'll be running along.

PETER. Thank you, Medford.

MEDFORD. Constable.

PETER. Constable.

MEDFORD. Well, good night, Sir Peter.

PETER. Good night, constable.

MEDFORD. Good night miss . . . er . . .

PETER. Vionysse.

MEDFORD. Well, good night. (*He starts to leave, for-
getting his truncheon.*) Oh, Sir Peter.

PETER. Yes.

MEDFORD. Do be careful about changing your plans,
sir. You never know but what other people might
change theirs. (*Exit.*)

PETER. Infuriating.

VIOLA. What a cheek, barging in here like that. The
London policeman's not what he used to be, you know.

PETER. The London policeman's not even what he seems to be.

VIOLA. Where were we?

PETER. Struggling.

VIOLA. Why don't you put out the lights again.

PETER. Why don't you ring the bell instead?

VIOLA. All right, does that bring the butler? (*Ring.*)

PETER. That's a matter for conjecture.

VIOLA. I beg your pardon.

PETER. Nothing.

VIOLA. We keep getting interrupted. Rose says when that happens the fates are against you.

PETER. It's not the fates I'm concerned about. It's the servant problem.

VIOLA. Rose says the servant problem's out of date.

PETER. Rose may very well be right. (MEDFORD *enters.*)

MEDFORD. Sir?

PETER. Run and fetch that policeman back, will you, Medford?

MEDFORD. Policeman, sir? Was there one here?

PETER. Yes, and I have unflagging faith in your ability to find him.

MEDFORD. Thank you, sir. (*Exits.*)

VIOLA. There's something familiar about him.

PETER. That's not the word.

VIOLA. I mean he looks like . . . or the policeman looks like . . . I must have had too much champagne.

PETER. Have some more.

VIOLA. Thank you. I love bubbles.

PETER. Another friend?

VIOLA. I mean in champagne.

PETER. Oh, I see.

VIOLA. You don't catch on very fast, do you?

PETER. I do my best.

VIOLA. Rose says that's all anyone can do. Their best. You know what I like most about Rose?

PETER. She carries a conversation?

VIOLA. Well, she always has something to say about . . . (MEDFORD *re-enters as policeman.*)

MEDFORD. You wanted me, Sir Peter?

PETER. Yes, I did.

MEDFORD. What can I do, Sir Peter? Anything the law can do to help the public, I'll be happy to do.

PETER. Then take your truncheon off my dining-table.

MEDFORD. Oh. Yes, sir, I am sorry about that. Didn't bust anything, did it?

PETER. Not yet it didn't.

MEDFORD. Well, good night, sir Peter. Good night, miss . . . er . . .

PETER. (*Firmly.*) Good night.

MEDFORD. Good night, all. (*Exits.*)

VIOLA. The food's cold.

PETER. That's a minor detail in the chaos of the evening.

VIOLA. Well, don't snap at me, for Heaven's sake.

PETER. I'm not snapping.

VIOLA. You're upset.

PETER. With very good cause.

VIOLA. Well, after all, he was only doing his duty.

PETER. He doesn't have to do it in my house.

VIOLA. He has to go where his duty takes him.

PETER. Yes, and it's going to take him further than he thinks.

VIOLA. How d'you know?

PETER. Because he's going to be fired tomorrow.

VIOLA. Who?

PETER. The boot-boy.

VIOLA. Who's he?

PETER. Medford.

VIOLA. I thought he was the butler.

PETER. *Was* is the operative word.

VIOLA. What are you talking about?

PETER. I haven't the faintest idea. Champagne?

VIOLA. Don't mind if I do.

PETER. What?

VIOLA. YES.

PETER. Yes what?

VIOLA. Yes I'd like some more champagne.

PETER. Well, why didn't you say so. There.

VIOLA. Thank you. Well, cheerio.

PETER. You're leaving?

VIOLA. No, that's just a toast, silly.

PETER. It certainly is.

VIOLA. What?

PETER. Silly.

VIOLA. Let's drink to us, then.

PETER. That's nearly as silly, but a little more appropriate.

VIOLA. Here's to us, alone and in love. (*They start to drink and* LADY ALEXANDRA *comes in dressed in Salvation Army uniform, beating on a tambourine and singing.*)

ALEX.

Turn away from shame and sorrow,
It may be too late tomorrow,
When the devil has you down below.

PETER. I knew the alone part wouldn't hold true.

ALEX. (*This speech should give the impression of being done in one breath.*) Sir Peter Tanford? How do you do? Well? Good! I'm Sergeant Penelope. And you want to know what I'm doing here, don't you? That's right, I knew you did. And do you know what my answer is? Of course, you don't. But you can guess,

can't you? You're nearly right. Are you doing your
part in what we, in the Salvation Army, call, and quite
appropriately I must say, for lack of a better term,
the good fight? Are you? Not really, you're not, are
you? No, I didn't think so. You want to do better,
don't you? You can, can't you? There I knew you
could. Well done! Now what I, a mere minion in the
great struggle, propose is this. Stop guessing. Prove
yourself, Sir Peter. How you ask? I'll tell you. Did
you know? Of course you didn't or you'd have been
out there fight, fight, fighting the good fight, wouldn't
you? Yes, Jolly Good! As I was saying before I tripped
over a loose clause, as I was saying, you just don't
know—how could you?—the awful, quite shockingly
sinful, predicament of many, many poor lost souls in
this, unfortunately immoral world. There are, and this
is not a genteel topic, there are, to let sex rear its all
too ugly head, women, who, if I may make so bold,
are, due entirely to unforseen circumstances, having,
or have had, or indeed are soon to have babies out of
wedlock. There I've said it! Don't you think that's
shocking? Yes, I knew you would. You recoil. I don't
wonder. And you who must be, unless I'm mistook,
Lady Sir Peter, and very charming and nice too—glad
to meet you, rather young but never mind, you must
be just melting, simply awash with compassion for
these girls who are, and I hesitate to say it, its nature
being, as you might say, unmentionable, and I am
indeed going to mention the unmentionable, who are
lured by, forgive me Sir Peter, men, to their, all too
often unhappy downfall. In short, and I like to make,
I say this humbly of course, my visits, if such you can
call, as well you may, fly-by-night meetings, visits,
brief, there's a problem. In, as it were, a nutshell, what
are we going to do for the little bastards? You're going

to help. If I may say so, Sir Peter, that's jolly white of you. A cheque! How personal. The Lord moves in a pecuniary way. I always say at our meetings, every Wednesday night, you might like them, come next week, that the British peerage are good fellows at heart. A hundred pounds will be fine. Thank you for volunteering. Sign right here. Not there. Here. Thank you, Sir Peter. Damn good show! The primrose path of immorality always leads slap into the stinging nettles. Don't you agree? I knew you would! Is there anything else you'd like to say? Good. It's not a thing to talk about, is it? No, it's not. Well, that, as they say, is that. Make that your last bottle of champagne. Remember sour grapes don't save a soul. The course of true love never did run smoothly down a dead end. You're a jolly good sort. Thank you once again. I am, to put it coarsely, off. Once more unto the breach! Down with the devil! Fight the good fight! You've done a wonderful thing for illegitimacy, Sir Peter. And so, good night. (*Exits singing. Pause.*)

VIOLA. What was that?

PETER. That was my wife.

VIOLA. What?

PETER. I said that sounded like my wife.

VIOLA. You poor thing. Aren't you glad she's not here?

PETER. Ecstatic. Champagne?

VIOLA. Thank you. I'm getting tiddly. I wonder what my mum would say, if she could see me now.

PETER. Nothing constructive.

VIOLA. (*Laughing gaily.*) I don't know, she's had eleven children.

PETER. How depressing.

VIOLA. Oh, no. She loves it.

PETER. Apparently.

VIOLA. How many children have you had?

PETER. Two boys.

VIOLA. That's nice.

PETER. Yes.

VIOLA. Is your wife pretty?

PETER. I find her quite remarkably beautiful. (*Slight pause.*)

VIOLA. You know what we need?

PETER. A lock on the door?

VIOLA. Music! Rose says music expresses people. She says if music be the food of love, let's have it. Isn't that good?

PETER. For Rose a little better than usual.

VIOLA. You ought to have some sort of stereophonic system where you just push a button and out comes music. You know, background noise.

PETER. Why don't we just sit quietly.

VIOLA. Doing what?

PETER. Whatever you like.

VIOLA. Ooh, you are naughty. (*Elaborately.*) Well, I'm at your mercy, Sir Peter.

PETER. Don't worry, I'll spare you.

VIOLA. Well, in that case, I'd certainly like some music. (*Immediately there is the sound of gypsy violins playing old-fashioned music badly.*) Ooh, what did you do?

PETER. Nothing to deserve this. (MEDFORD, *dressed as a Ruritanian gypsy violinist, comes into the room, singing.*)

MEDFORD.
I'll play a little gypsy song,
It's rather sweet and not too long,
A song from out your memory,
A half forgotten melody
   Of love

VIOLA. Oh, lovely.

PETER. To what, pray, do I owe this unsought for, unmusical interlude?

MEDFORD. Now, now, don't be a naughty boy, Sir Peter. I always serenade your weekly amours at this time on a Thursday evening. Three shillings a waltz, mazurka's extra, a little champagne, candles, and I leave the *"piece de resistance"* to you.

PETER. What the devil!

VIOLA. (*To* PETER.) Yes, what the devil!

MEDFORD. Madamoiselle is new?

VIOLA. Madamoiselle is getting older by the minute.

PETER. Hear, hear.

VIOLA. And what do you mean by that?

MEDFORD. Madamoiselle is not used to Sir Peter, yet. Always naughty, naughty little jokes. For shame, Sir Peter, to upset so fresh and charming a flower. A very lily of innocence. Uncontaminated by the cruel world that has made of me what you see of me. A prostitute . . .

VIOLA. I am not!

MEDFORD. I meant me. A prostitute of those rich, rare talents that once I used only for art's sake and that I now, perforce, must sell.

PETER. We don't want any.

MEDFORD. And you, Madamoiselle, blushing violet, and still Sir Peter, the naughtiest knight in London, must have his naughty little jests with her.

PETER. Mind you don't get your naughty little fiddle unstrung.

MEDFORD. You see, Madamoiselle, how this callous knight errant speaks to me, a prince in my own country and now, alas, a penniless exile forced to use my simple divine talents to serenade the seamier sides of society. Oh, dear, shall I continue?

VIOLA. Yes, play something.

PETER. I advise against it.

MEDFORD. I have polkas from Germany, minuets from France, and waltzes—divine, adorable waltzes—from dear old Vienna.

PETER. Why don't you return them?

MEDFORD. Monsieur does not appreciate music?

PETER. Monsieur does.

VIOLA. Can you play anything modern?

MEDFORD. Alas, no, sweet child, this foolish heart stopped beating when I was forced to flee my palace by an uninvited mob of sweating peasants who had just inopportunely discovered that they had a right to eat. And now my failing fingers play only echoes of a more autocratic era.

VIOLA. How sad.

PETER. Medford's been reading *The Prisoner of Zenda* again.

MEDFORD. Sir?

PETER. My butler, I'm sure you know him.

MEDFORD. The handsome young man? Very promising.

PETER. Promise which he will doubtless fulfill elsewhere.

MEDFORD. Oh, surely not?

PETER. Positively yes.

VIOLA. Why don't you play?

PETER. I think that . . .

MEDFORD. Frederick Maximillian Gustav Wilhelm August Horatio Erloskvock, the forty-second. You may call me Freddy.

PETER. . . . is played out.

MEDFORD. Not one pretty, little, tiny Tarantella?

PETER. Not one fleeting Flamenco.

VIOLA. Oh, yes.

MEDFORD. For Madamoiselle. (*He starts to play.*)

PETER. This is insufferable. Get out!

MEDFORD. Alas, his lordship is indisposed to music tonight. I make my adieus taking the food of love with me and leaving you to simpler fare. I wish you a rhapsodic evening. 'Night, 'night and don't be naughty. I shall fiddle elsewhere. (*Exits.*)

VIOLA. You were awfully rude.

PETER. I consider my behavior this evening to have been a model of self-restraint.

VIOLA. Well, you didn't have to treat him as if he were beneath contempt.

PETER. Whatever he may be beneath, I'll find him.

VIOLA. I wanted to hear some music. I'm not having a very nice time.

PETER. Neither am I.

VIOLA. Well, I like that!

PETER. I don't.

VIOLA. It's certainly not my fault. Rose warned me against people like you. Dull was what Rose said and Rose was right. I suppose you thought I was like all the others. Just because you're a knight doesn't mean a thing to me. What do you say to that?

PETER. (*Sincerely.*) I'm sorry.

VIOLA. I beg your pardon?

PETER. I said I am sorry.

VIOLA. (*Mollified.*) Well, of course, you're a gentleman. Rose said you were. And Rose was right.

PETER. A dull gentleman. Champagne?

VIOLA. It's nearly empty.

PETER. So it is.

VIOLA. And flat.

PETER. Yes.

VIOLA. Let's dance.

PETER. There's no music.

VIOLA. Well, we'll pretend. We've got to do something. Come on, it'll be lovely. (*She drags him up.*) I love dancing, don't you? (*They dance.*)

PETER. I used to.

VIOLA. We'll do that waltz in the show.

PETER. You're leading.

VIOLA. Sorry. Why don't you dip me. (*He dips her as* LADY ALEXANDRA, *disguised as a very old woman, pushes* MEDFORD, *as a very old man sitting in a wheelchair, into the room. The following sequence should be rapid and polished, not muddy.*)

ALEX. Peter! My darling boy! (PETER *drops* VIOLA, *who screams.*)

PETER. What in the name of . . .

ALEX. Surprise!

PETER. And who the hell are you now?

VIOLA. Help me up.

ALEX. That's a disgusting thing to say to your mother.

MEDFORD. What?

VIOLA. Help me up.

PETER. I'm going insane.

ALEX. Oh, darling no. You've got to come to dinner tomorrow.

VIOLA. Will somebody help me up?

PETER. Oh, shut up.

MEDFORD. What? (VIOLA *gets up.*)

PETER. I wasn't talking to you.

VIOLA. Who?

MEDFORD. What?

ALEX. Where's Alex? Who's this? And what's going on here?

MEDFORD. Pretty young filly. What?

VIOLA. How dare you!

ALEX. Oh, shut up!

MEDFORD. What?

VIOLA. Who?

PETER. You.

ALEX. Who?

VIOLA. Who are these people?

ALEX. (*Grande Dame.*) We are Peter's parents.

PETER. Oh, God!

VIOLA. His parents!

PETER. That's my mother, the Countess. And the paralytic idiot in the wheelchair is my dead father, the late Earl of Thring.

MEDFORD. What?

ALEX. Peter, how dare you!

PETER. How dare I?

ALEX. Yes.

PETER. How dare you?

MEDFORD. Who's the filly? Knew a girl like that in Calcutta. What?

VIOLA. (*Screaming.*) I am not a filly!

PETER. Oh, shut up!

VIOLA. How dare you!

ALEX. Who is this girl?

PETER. (*Together.*) Avis Phelps.

VIOLA. Viola Vionysse.

ALEX. But who is she?

PETER. I should have thought it was perfectly apparent.

MEDFORD. What?

VIOLA. Wait till I tell Rose about this.

ALEX. Rose who?

PETER. Her friend.

ALEX. Who is this girl?

MEDFORD. Damn pretty. Just like a girl in Rangoon. What?

VIOLA. I am not this girl. I've got a name.

ALEX. What is it?

PETER. (*Together.*) Avis Phelps.

VIOLA. Viola Vionysse. You're the rudest person I've known.

PETER. Who?

VIOLA. You.

ALEX. Who is this girl?

VIOLA. Listen, lady . . .

ALEX. Countess.

VIOLA. I don't care.

ALEX. I do.

MEDFORD. I remember one evening in Ranchipur. What?

VIOLA. Well, you're the rudest person I've ever met in my whole life.

PETER. How dare you speak to my wife like that.

VIOLA. That's your mother!

PETER. How do you know?

VIOLA. She just told me.

PETER. Well, she's wrong.

VIOLA. Don't shout at me.

PETER. This is my house and I shall shout at whomever I choose.

VIOLA. Just don't expect me to listen. (LADY ALEXANDRA *and* MEDFORD *watch, very amused.*)

PETER. I don't care if you listen or not. I intend to shout for my own amusement.

VIOLA. You're living in an insane asylum.

PETER. This is how I always spend my evenings. You must come more often.

VIOLA. I wouldn't come here again for a million pounds. (LADY ALEXANDRA *and* MEDFORD *quietly leave.*)

PETER. You won't be asked.

VIOLA. Rose always said never go where you're not wanted.

PETER. I'm tired of hearing all the silly things you've learnt from Rose. Next time you go somewhere why don't you leave the wretched girl at home.

VIOLA. I've had a horrible time.

PETER. It's not what I'd imagined either.

VIOLA. And you're not what I imagined. You're old, and dull, and boring, and rude. I had my dreams too. And they've all gone wrong because of you. Why didn't you ask someone else? Why me? I'm going home. On a double-decker bus. (*Exits. Pause.* PETER *goes to the table for champagne but it is empty. There is a knock at the door.* PETER *ignores it. Another knock. He ignores it.* LADY ALEXANDRA, *as herself in a long, comfortable dressing gown, comes in.*)

ALEX. Am I interrupting anything? (*Pause.*) How was your evening?

PETER. (*Slowly.*) Thanks to the intervention of you and that soon to be fired Medford, it was sheer unmitigated bloody hell, and I'm divorcing you tomorrow morning.

ALEX. Don't be silly, Noddy, after all that champagne you'll sleep till one. You always do.

PETER. After the embarrassment of the evening, I find this attempt at light social charm singularly ill-advised.

ALEX. But I'm not dressed to be serious.

PETER. You could be perched on top of Nelson's column in mid-winter wearing nothing but a topaz tiara for all I'd care.

ALEX. Don't be vulgar, Noddy.

PETER. This catastrophic misalliance is going to be terminated tomorrow. I can't possibly conceive why I married you in the first place.

ALEX. Our parents thought it would be a good idea.

PETER. That's the best argument I know against old age.

ALEX. (*Sweetly.*) Would you like me to give you grounds?

PETER. I don't want you to give me a damn thing.

ALEX. For divorce, darling. I imagine the simplest way is for one of us to have a rather torrid affair.

PETER. You seem to be taking this all very calmly.

ALEX. I never could stand scenes. They upset me. Well, shall I?

PETER. Shall you what?

ALEX. Give you grounds.

PETER. For divorce?

ALEX. Yes.

PETER. No.

ALEX. Why not? Moira Temple never has the slightest difficulty. She told me so, this evening. And Rodney Howard made ridiculous propositions all night long. I think I'll phone him.

PETER. You'll do no such thing.

ALEX. Why not?

PETER. I think it would be much better if you divorced me.

ALEX. For what?

PETER. Infidelity.

ALEX. But you haven't been.

PETER. Well, lie about it. For Heaven's sake, Alex, use your imagination.

ALEX. It's not lack of imagination; it's fear of perjury. The simplest thing is really for me to phone Rodney Howard.

PETER. That old lecher.

ALEX. Don't worry about it. It'll all go very smoothly. I'm sure he'll pick me up tonight.

PETER. I've decided you can divorce me. It's settled.

ALEX. Certainly not. Rodney Howard's very rich.

PETER. He's fat!

ALEX. He's not fat. He's a little plump. (*Laughing.*) And he owns a castle.

PETER. So what!

ALEX. He says it isn't difficult to keep clean at all.

PETER. (*Livid.*) Where were you? (LADY ALEXANDRA *is laughing helplessly.*) Where were you, Alex?

ALEX. Under the table. You kicked me.

PETER. Not hard enough!

ALEX. You know the earring she dropped?

PETER. (*Savagely.*) Intimately!

ALEX. I gave her one of mine instead.

PETER. What!

ALEX. I wonder what she'll make of that.

PETER. It's not funny.

ALEX. Of course it is.

PETER. (*He starts to see the funny side.*) You've reduced the whole evening to a Boulevard Farce.

ALEX. Better Boulevard Farce than domestic drama. Well, I'd better phone Rodney. It's getting late.

PETER. What on earth for?

ALEX. Grounds, darling.

PETER. If I ever so much as see you talking to Rodney Howard, I'll horsewhip you both.

ALEX. How very Victorian. Why should you care?

PETER. Because you're my wife, and, damn it, I love you. (*Pause.*)

ALEX. (*Slowly.*) Well, I'm glad that after twenty-five years you've made up your mind.

PETER. Twenty-five years?

ALEX. Yes. It's our anniversary. (*She rings. Immediately* MEDFORD *enters with a bottle of champagne.*)

MEDFORD. Supper, Sir Peter?

PETER. Yes, thank you, Medford.

MEDFORD. Champagne?

PETER. Thank you.

ALEX. Why, Noddy, this is the last bottle of the case I was given when I was married. How thoughtful of you.

PETER. Who gave you that champagne?

ALEX. Rodney Howard. When he was thin and rich.

PETER. I won't touch a drop of it.

ALEX. Don't be silly, Noddy. After all, I married you. He just thought he wanted me. He's really panting after some showgirl called Rose.

PETER. He never did have any taste.

MEDFORD. Is that all, Sir Peter?

PETER. Yes, thank you, Medford.

MEDFORD. Good night, Sir Peter. Lady Alexandra. Happy Anniversary. (*Exits.*)

PETER. Whatever are we going to do with Medford?

ALEX. Whatever would we do without him? (*They laugh.*)

PETER. Champagne?

ALEX. Thank you.

PETER. How was the party?

ALEX. Rather dull. Everyone was talking about their affairs, so, of course, I had to invent mine. I had a spectacular, if fictional, fling with the Duke of Dorset.

PETER. He's got gout.

ALEX. Only in his foot. (LADY ALEXANDRA *and* SIR PETER *talk quietly at the table. Big Ben begins to chime midnight.*)

CURTAIN

PROPERTY LIST

Ice-bucket
Champagne (2)
Champagne glasses (2)
Etiquette book
Silverware
Service plates (2)
Soup bowls (2)
Small soup tureen
Earrings—gaudy (Viola)
Earrings—expensive (Alexandra)
Candles
Flashlight (Policeman)
Truncheon (Policeman)
Hand bell on table (or a pull rope in room)
Tambourine (Penelope)
Check book and pen (Peter)
Violin (Gypsy) or use a concertina or accordion
Ear trumpet (Peter's Father)
Lap rug (Peter's Father)
Lorgnette (Peter's Mother)
Wheelchair—prefferably old-fashioned
Covered dishes on the sideboard (optional)
Flowers (optional)

COSTUME PLOT

SIR PETER
 Black dinner jacket, black tie, etc.
VIOLA
 Cocktail dress, a bit too flashy
LADY ALEXANDRA
 Full length evening gown
 Full length robe (or revert to evening gown)
MEDFORD
 Formal butler's outfit, with tail coat

DISGUISES

 Policeman (MEDFORD) traditional English policeman's outfit. Could use a black cape in lieu of
 tunic.

 Penelope (ALEXANDRA) traditional Salvation Army
 outfit—black with a bonnet.

 Gypsy (MEDFORD) his basic trousers and shirt,
 colourful sash at waist, scarf around head, large
 gold earring.

Peter's Mother (ALEXANDRA) almost anything, but
 old-fashioned furs or a cape, and wildly flowered
 hat might be nice.

 Peter's Father (MEDFORD) almost anything, but a
 blazer, straw boater and a walrus moustache
 would do. Cravat, ear trumpet, lap rug.

The disguise costumes need not be very authentic as
they are supposed to be improvised.

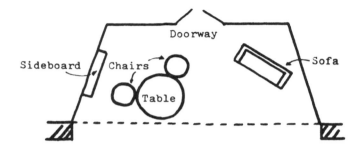

PASTICHE

All that is essential is an entrance,
a table and two chairs. The table should
be on castors or wheels and covered with
a floor-length tablecloth.

38

OTHER TITLES AVAILABLE FROM SAMUEL FRENCH

NO SEX PLEASE, WE'RE BRITISH
Anthony Marriott and Alistair Foot

Farce / 7 m, 3 f / Interior

A young bride who lives above a bank with her husband who is the assistant manager, innocently sends a mail order off for some Scandinavian glassware. What comes is Scandinavian pornography. The plot revolves around what is to be done with the veritable floods of pornography, photographs, books, films and eventually girls that threaten to engulf this happy couple. The matter is considerably complicated by the man's mother, his boss, a visiting bank inspector, a police superintendent and a muddled friend who does everything wrong in his reluctant efforts to set everything right, all of which works up to a hilarious ending of closed or slamming doors. This farce ran in London over eight years and also delighted Broadway audiences.

"Titillating and topical."
– NBC TV

"A really funny Broadway show."
– ABC TV

THE DECORATOR
Donald Churchill

Comedy / 1m, 2f / Interior

Marcia returns to her flat to find it has not been painted as she arranged. A part time painter who is filling in for an ill colleague is just beginning the work when the wife of the man with whom Marcia is having an affair arrives to tell all to Marcia's husband. Marcia hires the painter a part time actor to impersonate her husband at the confrontation. Hilarity is piled upon hilarity as the painter, who takes his acting very seriously, portrays the absent husband. The wronged wife decides that the best revenge is to sleep with Marcia's husband, an ecstatic experience for them both. When Marcia learns that the painter/actor has slept with her rival, she demands the opportunity to show him what really good sex is.

"Irresistible."
– *London Daily Telegraph*

"This play will leave you rolling in the aisles....
I all but fell from my seat laughing."
– *London Star*

PERFECT WEDDING
Robin Hawdon

Comedy / 2m, 4f / Interior

A man wakes up in the bridal suite on his wedding morning to find an extremely attractive naked girl in bed beside him. In the depths of a stag night hangover, he can't even remember meeting her. Before he can get her out, his bride to be arrives to dress for the wedding. In the ensuing panic, the girl is locked in the bathroom. The best man is persuaded to claim her, but he gets confused and introduces the chamber maid to the bride as his date. The crisis escalates to nuclear levels by the time the mother of the bride and the best man's actual girlfriend arrive. This rare combination of riotous farce and touching love story has provoked waves of laughter across Europe and America.

"Laughs abound."
– *Wisconsin Advocate*

"The full house audience roared with delight."
– *Green Bay Gazette*

Lightning Source UK Ltd.
Milton Keynes UK
UKOW06f0757100216

268073UK00001B/20/P

9 780573 624261